Terrific Toddlers

Boo-Boo!

by Carol Zeavin, MSEd, MEd
and Rhona Silverbush, JD

illustrated by Jon Davis

Magination Press • Washington, DC • American Psychological Association

Magination Press

American Psychological Association
750 First Street NE
Washington, DC 20002

With gratitude to my inspiring teachers and mentors at Bank Street, Rockefeller, and Barnard—*CZ*
Dedicated to the inspiration for this series, with infinite love—*RS*
For Laura and Greta—*JD*

Magination Press is a registered trademark of the American Psychological Association.
Order books here: www.apa.org/pubs/magination or 1-800-374-2721

Book design by Gwen Grafft
Printed by Worzalla, Stevens Point, WI

Library of Congress Cataloging-in-Publication Data
Names: Zeavin, Carol, author. | Silverbush, Rhona, 1967 – author. | Davis,
    Jon, 1969 – illustrator.
Title: Boo-boo! / by Carol Zeavin, MSEd, MEd, and Rhona Silverbush, JD ;
    illustrated by Jon Davis.
Description: Washington, DC : Magination Press, an imprint of the American
    Psychological Association, [2018] | Series: Terrific toddlers | Audience: Age 2–3.
Identifiers: LCCN 2017038181| ISBN 9781433828751 (hardcover) |
    ISBN 1433828758 (hardcover)
Subjects: LCSH: Children—Wounds and injuries—Juvenile literature.
Classification: LCC RD93.5.C4 Z43 2018 | DDC 617.10083—dc23 LC record
    available at https://lccn.loc.gov/2017038181

Manufactured in the United States of America
10 9 8 7 6 5 4 3 2 1

Sometimes we get boo-boos!
Sometimes boo-boos hurt, and sometimes they are scary.

Here comes JoJo.
JoJo likes to run FAST!

She is running, running, running down the block.
Uh-oh! JoJo falls down and bumps her chin.

JoJo gets a boo-boo!

JoJo cries. Daddy picks her up.
"You fell down. Are you OK?"
Daddy says, "Ouch, that hurt your chin."
JoJo wails, "A boo-boo!"

Daddy kisses JoJo's boo-boo.
"Come, let's fix your boo-boo."

JoJo cries harder.
"No fix! No fix!"

Daddy says, "I see you're scared. I'll help you. We need to wash your boo-boo."

JoJo cries louder. "No wash! No wash!"

"I know it hurts. Let's wash and count to ten..."
"...eight...nine...ten! And now
a Band-Aid on your chin."

JoJo screams, "No Band-Aid!"

Daddy asks, "Does Daddy
have a boo-boo, too?"
JoJo puts a Band-Aid on...
Daddy's nose!
Daddy looks silly.

JoJo cries and smiles
at the same time.

Daddy says, "Your turn!"

JoJo isn't crying anymore.
"JoJo Band-Aid. Daddy Band-Aid."

Daddy says, "You fell
down and got a boo-boo.
Then you cried.
And now you're OK."

"I OK, Daddy!"

Boo-boos get better!

Note to Parents and Caregivers

We know they're low to the ground, but with their high energy levels and fearless explorations, toddlers sure are prone to injury. Most such injuries are minor—cuts, scrapes, and scratches—so we adults just want to clean and bandage them quickly, with a minimum of fuss. If only our toddlers would let us!

But to a toddler, even a small cut, scrape, or scratch is a big deal. After all, toddlers don't yet know that the injury will repair itself. It's an assault on their growing, but as yet fragile, sense of wholeness. They think they're broken forever.

And sometimes, no matter how uncomfortable the injury, toddlers are likely to consider the cure to be worse. "No Band-Aid!"* But once a toddler has come to understand that Band-Aids are not the enemy, the Band-Aid becomes the cure-all. Covering the wounded area makes the toddler feel whole again.

Your best bets?

1. **Acknowledge and validate your child's fear.** Toddlerhood is the time, through about age 5, when children start to have a lot of seemingly irrational fears. Never ignore or dismiss a fear, no matter how irrational it may seem to you. Your child is really afraid, and the adult's denial or minimization will not only increase the fear, but can add an unnecessary layer of distrust into the mix. Respect for children's concerns helps them master their fears and anxieties—a skill set that will serve them well throughout life!

2. **Keep a calm tone and demeanor.** At the same time, maintain your own emotional equilibrium. Your child will look to you, your tone and demeanor, for an indication of how serious the injury is. Acknowledging your toddler's genuine feelings of shock and hurt, without becoming part of them, helps your toddler gain a similar perspective.

3. **Use distractions.** After acknowledging your child's fear, you can use fun, silly distractions that may lighten the mood. These diversions should engage the senses, which is where a young child lives: use visuals ("Daddy gets a Band-Aid!"), gentle touch (on a non-injured area!), sound (familiar songs, soothing humming), whatever helps your child move through the hurt and back to real life.

*A word about JoJo's pronunciation: Please don't worry if your toddler can't say "wash" or "Band-Aid" as well as JoJo! JoJo can't say them, either, we just didn't want you to have to decipher words with missing letters or confusing spellings ("Band-Aid" might sound more like "ban-ee," and "wash" may sound like "wahs"). If you wish to know more about your toddler's development of speech sounds, you can refer to speech sounds development charts on the web, for example: https://childdevelopment.com.au/resources/child-development-charts/speech-sounds-developmental-chart/

Carol Zeavin holds master's degrees in education and special education from Bank Street College, worked with infants and toddlers for nearly a decade as head teacher at Rockefeller University's Child and Family Center and Barnard's Toddler Development Center, and worked at Y.A.I. and Theracare. She lives in New York, NY.

Rhona Silverbush studied psychology and theater at Brandeis University and law at Boston College Law School. She represented refugees and has written and co-written several books, including a guide to acting Shakespeare. She currently coaches actors, writes, tutors, and consults for families of children and teens with learning differences and special needs. She lives in New York, NY.

Jon Davis is an award-winning illustrator of more than 70 books. He lives in England.